What's in this book

This book belongs to

_____

新同学 New schoolmates

学习内容 Contents

沟通 Communication

说说位置
Talk about locations

生词 New words

★	新	new
★	旧	old
★	左边	left
★	右边	right
★	桌子	desk
★	但是	but
★	妹妹	younger sister
	班	class
	年级	grade
	教室	classroom
	椅子	chair
	找	to look for

背景介绍:
学校来了新同学,浩浩和小伙伴们
都好奇地看着他们。

大卫想去找妹妹，但是他不知道她在哪里。

David wants to find his younger sister but he doesn't know where she is.

参考答案：

1 Yes, Peter and Sally have just come to my school./ No, I don't.
2 I introduce myself to them./I ask for their names.
3 Yes, I think they do because they look interested in them./They are curious about the new schoolmates but I cannot tell if they like them.

文化 Cultures

中国的初等教育
Primary education in China

跨学科学习 Project

比较电脑教室
Compare computer classrooms

Get ready

1 Do you have any new schoolmates?

2 What do you do when you meet new schoolmates?

3 Do you think Hao Hao and his friends like the new schoolmates?

bān
班

xīn
新

故事大意：
班级上来了一个转校生。同学们对他很好奇，他有不熟悉的地方都向他介绍，体现了同学间的互助互爱。

参考问题和答案：
1 What is Ms Wu doing? (She is introducing a new classmate to the class.)
2 What do you think the new classmate is saying? (He is saying "Good morning, everyone. My name is David. I am your new classmate.)

班上来了一个新同学，他叫大卫。大家都很喜欢他。

参考问题和答案：

1. Where is David seated in relation to Hao Hao? (He is in front of Hao Hao.)
2. For Hao Hao, is Elsa on the left or right side of David? (She is on the left.)
3. For Hao Hao, is Ivan on the left or right side of David? (He is on the right side of David.)
4. Is your class seated similar to this class? (Yes./No, we sit in small groups.)

zuǒ biān
左边

yòu biān
右边

大卫坐在浩浩的前面，他的左边是爱莎，右边是艾文。

提醒学生视觉是从课室后面看过去的。

参考问题和答案：

1 Why are the children playing in the corridor? (Because it is recess.)
2 What does David want to do? (He wants to find his younger sister.)
3 Does he know where to find her? (He does not. He looks puzzled.)

mèi mei
妹妹

dàn shì
但是

"但是"用在后半句，
表示转折的语气。

zhǎo
找

下课了，大卫想去找妹妹，但是他
不知道她在哪里。

年级
nián jí

Grade 1 一年级

参考问题和答案：
1 What is Hao Hao doing? (He is taking David to his younger sister.)
2 Where are they going? (They are going to a Grade 1 classroom.)

"我们带你去。"大家说。
"谢谢！她读一年级。"大卫说。

参考问题和答案：

1 Has David found his younger sister? (Yes, he has. She is in her classroom.)
2 Is this classroom the same as David's? (No, it is different.)
3 What are Hao Hao and his friends doing? (They are looking at the classroom.)

jiào shì
教室

"哥哥，我在这里！"大卫妹妹说。
"你的教室真可爱。"大卫说。

"旧"的反义词是"新"。

jiù
旧

参考问题和答案：

1 What is Hao Hao explaining to David and his sister?
   (He is saying that this classroom is his 'old' classroom.)
2 Are the tables and the chairs the same as before? (Yes, they are.)

zhuō zi
桌子

yǐ zi
椅子

"这是我们的旧教室，桌子、椅子还
是和以前一样。"大家说。

Let's think

1 Recall the story. Put a tick or a cross.

2 There are many different classroom seating plans. Can you draw yours?

告诉学生小图中的"T"表示老师，"S"表示学生。学生画完后，可以让学生说说更喜欢哪一种座位分布情况。

New words

🎧 02 **1** Learn the new words.

延伸活动：
学生几人一组，利用刚学到的生词和已有中文知识，对自己的课室进行描述。

参考表述： 我很喜欢我的教室，因为它很好看。教室的门上写了三年级A班。教室里，桌子是黄色的，椅子是蓝色的。我左边和右边的同学都是我的好朋友。

年级　班

新

旧

一年级A班

左边

右边

但是

妹妹

椅子

找

桌子

教室

2 Say the words to your friend and ask him/her to point to the correct words in the picture above.

听听说说 Listen and say

第一题录音稿：
1 爸爸给我买了新衣服，我很高兴。
2 他叫大卫，是我的新同学，坐在我的前
3 她是大卫的妹妹，今年刚上一年级，她
  大卫小三岁。

03 **1** Listen and write the letters.

1 我喜欢我的 ___a___ ，
  它是爸爸给我的。

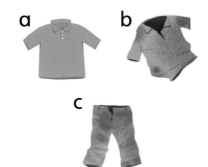

a   b

c

2 他是我的同学，坐
  在我的 ___b___ 边。

a   b

c

3 她是大卫的 ___a___ ，
  她比大卫小三岁。

a   b

c

04 **2** Look at the pictures. Listen to the story a

1

大卫，你怎么了？

我想去洗手间，但是不知道在哪里

3

在我妹妹教室的左边吗？

是的。

第二题参考问题和答案：

1 Does Elsa know her school well? (Yes, she does.)
2 Is she helpful to David? (Yes, she is.)
3 Do you like to help your schoolmates? (Yes, I always help others.)

ﬔy.

洗手间在一年级 A 班教室的左边。

4

那很好找。谢谢你，爱莎。

不客气！

3 **Write the letters and say.**

| a 左边 | b 右边 | c 但是 |
| d 新 | e 妹妹 | f 桌子 |

我有哥哥和姐姐，__c__ 我没有妹妹。

这是我和 __e__ 的卧室。我们的床在 __b__，__f__ 和椅子在 __a__。

这是我的 __d__ 雨伞，我很喜欢它的颜色。

13

Task

Paste or draw a picture of your classroom and talk about the classrooms with your friend.

你的教室怎么样？

这些新桌子和新椅子很好看。

这是旧教室。

我的教室……

Game

延伸游戏：
待学生熟悉这些方位词后，全班听老师随机说某一字，并做相应的动作，做错的学生被淘汰出游戏，最后剩下的一个学生为胜。

Say the words and act it out. Can you get them all right?

上

下

前

后

左

右

Chant

学生一边说唱，当唱到"学校"、"教室"、"桌子"、"椅子"、"年级"时，大家击掌两次。

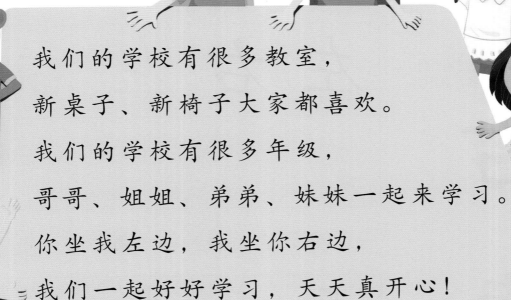

Listen and say.

我们的学校有很多教室，

新桌子、新椅子大家都喜欢。

我们的学校有很多年级，

哥哥、姐姐、弟弟、妹妹一起来学习。

你坐我左边，我坐你右边，

我们一起好好学习，天天真开心！

生活用语 Daily expressions

你找谁？

你找谁？
Who are you looking for?

我带你去。

我带你去。
I will take you there.

写一写 Write

1 Trace and write the characters.

一 ナ ナ 左 左
一 ナ 才 右 右

提醒学生注意"左"、"右"两字的左上方都是一样的,并不要混淆两字。

左	右	左	右

丨 卜 卜 占 占 卢 卓 卓 桌

桌	桌	桌	桌

"桌"是形声字,"木"表意,表示桌子用树木制成,"卓"表声。

2 Write and say.

男孩在小狗 __右__ 边。
小狗在男孩 __左__ 边。

这是我的床、__桌子__ 和椅子,
你喜欢吗?

提醒学生视角不同,答案也会不同。以上答案是从读者的角度来看;若从男孩角度看,则答案相反。

3 Fill in the blanks with the correct words. Colour the school bags using the same colours.

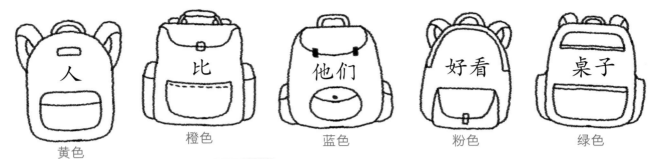

人
黄色

比
橙色

他们
蓝色

好看
粉色

桌子
绿色

<u>他们</u>是英国<u>人</u>。这是他们的教室。教室里的<u>桌子</u>和椅子是蓝色的。他们的教室<u>比</u>我们的教室<u>好看</u>吗？

拼音输入法 Pinyin input

To type Chinese faster, we can type the words with two or more characters all at one time.

1 Type the words using two ways. Tick the method which is faster.

同学

☑ tongxue

☐ tong xue

三明治

☐ san ming zhi

☑ sanmingzhi

新年

☑ xinnian

☐ xin nian

2 Write the Pinyin, then type the words. Can you get them all correct?

教室
jiaoshi

下雨
xiayu

巧克力
qiaokeli

多元学习 Connections

中国现行九年义务教育分为"五四制"和"六三制"。"五四制"即小学五年、初中四年；"六三制"即小学六年，初中三年。九年制义务教育不收学费和杂费，每个适龄儿童有权且必须接受义务教育。

1 What do primary students in China do at school? Is their school system different from yours?

In China, primary education is a part of the Nine-year Compulsory Education. It usually lasts for six years with two terms in each school year. All children must attend primary school at age 6 or 7.

2 Compare the subjects in schools in China with your school. Circle the ones which are different.

Primary school subjects in China

音乐 Music 　　数学 Mathematics

科学 Science 　　外语 Foreign Language

语文 Chinese 　　体育 PE (Physical Education)

美术 Arts 　　品德与社会 Moral Education and Social Studies

除以上课程外，信息技术 Information Technology 在学校里也越来越普及。

Project

向学生简单介绍：电子计算机，也叫作电脑，是根据一系列指令对资料进行处理的工具。电脑的发展有三百多年历史，今天，它已被应用于手机、电视、数位相机、游戏机等生活用品之中。

1 Paste a photo of your computer classroom below. Look at the photos and talk about the classrooms with your friend.

Paste your photo here.

我喜欢左边的电脑教室。

右边是我的电脑教室。

我喜欢这些桌子、椅子、电脑。

这些电脑……

四个同学坐在一起。

我喜欢在……

2 What lessons are the children having? Type the subjects in Chinese. Say to your friend.

数学

美术

音乐

鼓励学生用完整的句子描述这些图片，如：她喜欢画画，也很喜欢美术课。/他们的音乐课很好玩。/这是他们的教室，他们喜欢数学课。

温习 Checkpoint

1 Follow the arrows and complete the tasks in the classrooms. Then go to the main door and take the school bus home.

大卫想找妹妹，但是他不知道她在哪里。

爱莎在大卫的 左 边，艾文在大卫的 右 边。

Which grade are you in? Answer in Chinese.
我读……年级。

What is the name of your class? Answer in Chinese.
我在……班。

她是大卫的什么人？
她是大卫的妹妹。

他叫什么名字？
他叫大卫。

这是 桌 子。

这是新教室还是旧教室？ 这是旧教室。

→

这里的椅子是什么颜色的？ 这里的椅子是黄色和蓝色的。

延伸活动：

让学生互相说说自己学校的情况，如有几个年级、有多少个班、班上学生人数、课室数目等。参考表述包括：我的学校不大，有六个年级，一个年级有三个班，班里有20个同学。学校有28个教室。

评核方法：

学生两人一组，互相考察评价表内单词和句子的听说读写。交际沟通部分由老师朗读要求，学生再互相对话。如果达到了某项技能要求，则用色笔将星星或小辣椒涂色。

2 Work with your friend. Colour the stars and the chillies.

Words and sentences	说	读	写
新	☆	☆	🌶
旧	☆	☆	🌶
左边	☆	☆	☆
右边	☆	☆	☆
桌子	☆	☆	☆
但是	☆	☆	🌶
妹妹	☆	☆	🌶
班	☆	🌶	🌶
年级	☆	🌶	🌶
教室	☆	🌶	🌶
椅子	☆	🌶	🌶
找	☆	🌶	🌶
大卫想去找妹妹，但是他不知道她在哪里。	☆	☆	🌶

Talk about locations	☆

3 What does your teacher say?

评核建议：

根据学生课堂表现，分别给予"太棒了！(Excellent!)"、"不错！(Good!)"或"继续努力！(Work harder!)"的评价，再让学生圈出左侧对应的表情，以记录自己的学习情况。

分享 Sharing

Words I remember

新	xīn	new
旧	jiù	old
左边	zuǒ biān	left
右边	yòu biān	right
桌子	zhuō zi	table
但是	dàn shì	but
妹妹	mèi mei	younger sister
班	bān	class
年级	nián jí	grade
教室	jiào shì	classroom
椅子	yǐ zi	chair
找	zhǎo	to find

Other words

坐	zuò	to sit
想	xiǎng	to want to
带	dài	to take
读	dú	to read
以前	yǐ qián	before
品德	pǐn dé	Moral Education
社会	shè huì	Social Studies
科学	kē xué	Science
音乐	yīn yuè	Music
体育	tǐ yù	PE (Physical Education)
语文	yǔ wén	Chinese Language
外语	wài yǔ	Foreign Language

延伸活动：

1 学生用手遮盖英文，读中文单词，并思考单词意思；

2 学生用手遮盖中文单词，看着英文说出对应的中文单词；

3 学生三人一组，尽量运用中文单词分角色复述故事。

OXFORD
UNIVERSITY PRESS

Oxford University Press is a department of the University of Oxford.
It furthers the University's objective of excellence in research, scholarship,
and education by publishing worldwide. Oxford is a registered trade mark of
Oxford University Press in the UK and in certain other countries

Published in Hong Kong by
Oxford University Press (China) Limited
39th Floor, One Kowloon, 1 Wang Yuen Street, Kowloon Bay,
Hong Kong

© Oxford University Press (China) Limited 2017

Illustrated by Anne Lee, Emily Chan, KY Chan and Wildman

Photographs for reproduction permitted by Dreamstime.com

China National Publications Import & Export (Group) Corporation is an authorized distributor of
Oxford Elementary Chinese.

Please contact content@cnpiec.com.cn or 86-10-65856782

ISBN: 978-0-19-082254-5

10 9 8 7 6 5 4 3 2

Teacher's Edition
ISBN: 978-0-19-082266-8

10 9 8 7 6 5 4 3 2